This bucket list belongs to

____

Our Bucket List

IDEA

PAGE　WE DID IT!

Our Bucket List

IDEA	PAGE	WE DID IT!
		☐
		☐
		☐
		☐
		☐
		☐
		☐
		☐
		☐
		☐
		☐
		☐
		☐
		☐
		☐

Our Bucket List

IDEA   PAGE   WE DID IT!

Bucket List Idea

WHAT?

WHY?

We did it!

WHEN?

WHERE?

HOW WAS IT?

WOULD WE DO IT AGAIN?

Bucket List Idea

WHAT?

WHY?

We did it!

WHEN?

WHERE?

HOW WAS IT?

WOULD WE DO IT AGAIN?

Bucket List Idea

WHAT?

WHY?

We did it!

WHEN?

WHERE?

HOW WAS IT?

WOULD WE DO IT AGAIN?

Bucket List Idea

WHAT?

WHY?

We did it!

WHEN?

WHERE?

HOW WAS IT?

WOULD WE DO IT AGAIN?

Bucket List Idea

WHAT?

WHY?

We did it!

WHEN?

WHERE?

HOW WAS IT?

WOULD WE DO IT AGAIN?

Bucket List Idea

WHAT?

WHY?

We did it!

WHEN?

WHERE?

HOW WAS IT?

WOULD WE DO IT AGAIN?

Bucket List Idea

WHAT?

WHY?

We did it!

WHEN?

WHERE?

HOW WAS IT?

WOULD WE DO IT AGAIN?

Bucket List Idea

WHAT?

WHY?

We did it!

WHEN?

WHERE?

HOW WAS IT?

WOULD WE DO IT AGAIN?

Bucket List Idea

WHAT?

WHY?

We did it!

WHEN?

WHERE?

HOW WAS IT?

WOULD WE DO IT AGAIN?

Bucket List Idea

WHAT?

WHY?

We did it!

WHEN?

WHERE?

HOW WAS IT?

WOULD WE DO IT AGAIN?

WHAT?

WHY?

We did it!

WHEN?

WHERE?

HOW WAS IT?

WOULD WE DO IT AGAIN?

Bucket List Idea

WHAT?

WHY?

We did it!

WHEN?

WHERE?

HOW WAS IT?

WOULD WE DO IT AGAIN?

Bucket List Idea

WHAT?

WHY?

We did it!

WHEN?

WHERE?

HOW WAS IT?

WOULD WE DO IT AGAIN?

Bucket List Idea

WHAT?

WHY?

We did it!

WHEN?

WHERE?

HOW WAS IT?

WOULD WE DO IT AGAIN?

Bucket List Idea

WHAT?

WHY?

We did it!

WHEN?

WHERE?

HOW WAS IT?

WOULD WE DO IT AGAIN?

Bucket List Idea

WHAT?

WHY?

We did it!

WHEN?

WHERE?

HOW WAS IT?

WOULD WE DO IT AGAIN?

Bucket List Idea

WHAT?

WHY?

We did it!

WHEN?

WHERE?

HOW WAS IT?

WOULD WE DO IT AGAIN?

Bucket List Idea

WHAT?

WHY?

We did it!

WHEN?

WHERE?

HOW WAS IT?

WOULD WE DO IT AGAIN?

Bucket List Idea

WHAT?

WHY?

We did it!

WHEN?

WHERE?

HOW WAS IT?

WOULD WE DO IT AGAIN?

Bucket List Idea

WHAT?

WHY?

We did it!

WHEN?

WHERE?

HOW WAS IT?

WOULD WE DO IT AGAIN?

Bucket List Idea

WHAT?

WHY?

We did it!

WHEN?

WHERE?

HOW WAS IT?

WOULD WE DO IT AGAIN?

Bucket List Idea

WHAT?

WHY?

We did it!

WHEN?

WHERE?

HOW WAS IT?

WOULD WE DO IT AGAIN?

Bucket List Idea

WHAT?

WHY?

We did it!

WHEN?

WHERE?

HOW WAS IT?

WOULD WE DO IT AGAIN?

Bucket List Idea

WHAT?

____

____

____

____

____

WHY?

____

____

____

____

____

____

____

____

We did it!

WHEN?

WHERE?

HOW WAS IT?

WOULD WE DO IT AGAIN?

Bucket List Idea

WHAT?

WHY?

We did it!

WHEN?

WHERE?

HOW WAS IT?

WOULD WE DO IT AGAIN?

Bucket List Idea

WHAT?

WHY?

We did it!

WHEN?

WHERE?

HOW WAS IT?

WOULD WE DO IT AGAIN?

Bucket List Idea

WHAT?

WHY?

We did it!

WHEN?

WHERE?

HOW WAS IT?

WOULD WE DO IT AGAIN?

Bucket List Idea

WHAT?

WHY?

We did it!

WHEN?

WHERE?

HOW WAS IT?

WOULD WE DO IT AGAIN?

Bucket List Idea

WHAT?

WHY?

We did it!

WHEN?

WHERE?

HOW WAS IT?

WOULD WE DO IT AGAIN?

Bucket List Idea

WHAT?

WHY?

We did it!

WHEN?

WHERE?

HOW WAS IT?

WOULD WE DO IT AGAIN?

Bucket List Idea

WHAT?

WHY?

We did it!

WHEN?

WHERE?

HOW WAS IT?

WOULD WE DO IT AGAIN?

Bucket List Idea

WHAT?

WHY?

We did it!

WHEN?

WHERE?

HOW WAS IT?

WOULD WE DO IT AGAIN?

Bucket List Idea

WHAT?

WHY?

We did it!

WHEN?

WHERE?

HOW WAS IT?

WOULD WE DO IT AGAIN?

Bucket List Idea

WHAT?

WHY?

We did it!

WHEN?

WHERE?

HOW WAS IT?

WOULD WE DO IT AGAIN?

Bucket List Idea

WHAT?

WHY?

We did it!

WHEN?

WHERE?

HOW WAS IT?

WOULD WE DO IT AGAIN?

Bucket List Idea

WHAT?

____

____

____

____

____

WHY?

____

____

____

____

____

____

____

____

We did it!

WHEN?

WHERE?

HOW WAS IT?

WOULD WE DO IT AGAIN?

Bucket List Idea

WHAT?

WHY?

We did it!

WHEN?

WHERE?

HOW WAS IT?

WOULD WE DO IT AGAIN?

Bucket List Idea

WHAT?

WHY?

We did it!

WHEN?

WHERE?

HOW WAS IT?

WOULD WE DO IT AGAIN?

Bucket List Idea

WHAT?

WHY?

We did it!

WHEN?

WHERE?

HOW WAS IT?

WOULD WE DO IT AGAIN?

Bucket List Idea

WHAT?

WHY?

We did it!

WHEN?

WHERE?

HOW WAS IT?

WOULD WE DO IT AGAIN?

Bucket List Idea

WHAT?

WHY?

We did it!

WHEN?

WHERE?

HOW WAS IT?

WOULD WE DO IT AGAIN?

Bucket List Idea

WHAT?

WHY?

We did it!

WHEN?

WHERE?

HOW WAS IT?

WOULD WE DO IT AGAIN?

Bucket List Idea

WHAT?

WHY?

We did it!

WHEN?

WHERE?

HOW WAS IT?

WOULD WE DO IT AGAIN?

Bucket List Idea

WHAT?

WHY?

We did it!

WHEN?

WHERE?

HOW WAS IT?

WOULD WE DO IT AGAIN?

Bucket List Idea

WHAT?

WHY?

We did it!

WHEN?

WHERE?

HOW WAS IT?

WOULD WE DO IT AGAIN?